50 Keto Dessert Recipes for Home

By: Kelly Johnson

Table of Contents

- Keto Chocolate Avocado Pudding
- Almond Flour Chocolate Chip Cookies
- Keto Cheesecake Bites
- Coconut Flour Lemon Poppy Seed Muffins
- Avocado Chocolate Mousse
- Keto Chocolate Fat Bombs
- Sugar-Free Vanilla Ice Cream
- Chocolate Peanut Butter Keto Cups
- Keto Pumpkin Pie Bars
- Almond Butter Keto Brownies
- Keto Chocolate Covered Strawberries
- No-Bake Coconut Almond Energy Balls
- Keto Chocolate Mug Cake
- Raspberry Almond Chia Pudding
- Keto Almond Joy Fat Bombs
- Blueberry Coconut Flour Mug Cake
- Keto Chocolate Hazelnut Truffles
- Lemon Cheesecake Fat Bombs
- Chocolate Avocado Keto Ice Cream
- Keto Peanut Butter Cookies
- Pumpkin Spice Keto Fat Bombs
- Coconut Flour Chocolate Zucchini Bread
- Keto Chocolate Almond Bark
- Vanilla Coconut Flour Mug Cake
- Keto Chocolate Chip Cookie Dough Fat Bombs
- Strawberry Cheesecake Keto Fat Bombs
- Almond Flour Keto Donuts
- Chocolate Coconut Flour Pancakes
- Keto Chocolate Pecan Pie Bars
- Lemon Almond Flour Shortbread Cookies
- Keto Chocolate Peanut Butter Cups

- Coconut Flour Pumpkin Muffins
- Chocolate Mint Keto Fat Bombs
- Vanilla Almond Flour Cupcakes
- Keto Chocolate Macadamia Nut Cookies
- Avocado Lime Keto Cheesecake
- Peanut Butter Chocolate Chip Keto Blondies
- Almond Flour Berry Cobbler
- Keto Chocolate Mint Ice Cream
- Coconut Flour Chocolate Mug Cake
- Keto Pumpkin Spice Fat Bombs
- Raspberry Almond Flour Scones
- Keto Chocolate Avocado Truffles
- Almond Butter Keto Chocolate Fudge
- Blueberry Coconut Flour Pancakes
- Keto Almond Flour Waffles
- Chocolate Coconut Flour Cupcakes
- Keto Lemon Coconut Fat Bombs
- Pumpkin Pie Keto Chia Pudding
- Almond Flour Keto Cinnamon Rolls

Keto Chocolate Avocado Pudding

Ingredients:

- 2 ripe avocados, peeled and pitted
- 1/4 cup unsweetened cocoa powder
- 1/4 cup almond milk or coconut milk (unsweetened)
- 1/4 cup powdered erythritol or your preferred keto-friendly sweetener
- 1 teaspoon vanilla extract
- A pinch of salt
- Optional toppings: whipped cream, chopped nuts, or berries

Instructions:

Prepare the Avocados:
- Scoop out the flesh from the ripe avocados and place them in a blender or food processor.

Add Cocoa Powder:
- Add the unsweetened cocoa powder to the blender.

Pour in Almond Milk:
- Add the almond milk (or coconut milk) to the blender.

Sweeten It Up:
- Add the powdered erythritol (or your chosen sweetener) to the mixture.

Add Flavor:
- Pour in the vanilla extract and add a pinch of salt for flavor balance.

Blend Until Smooth:
- Blend all the ingredients until you achieve a smooth and creamy consistency. You may need to stop and scrape down the sides of the blender to ensure everything is well incorporated.

Taste and Adjust:
- Taste the pudding and adjust the sweetness or cocoa level according to your preference.

Chill:
- Transfer the chocolate avocado pudding to serving bowls or jars.
- Refrigerate for at least 1-2 hours to allow the pudding to chill and thicken.

Serve:

- Once chilled, you can serve the Keto Chocolate Avocado Pudding on its own or with optional toppings like whipped cream, chopped nuts, or berries.

Enjoy:
- Enjoy this rich and creamy chocolate pudding that's keto-friendly and packed with healthy fats from avocados.

This Keto Chocolate Avocado Pudding is not only delicious but also a great way to incorporate nutrient-rich avocados into your keto dessert. The avocados lend a creamy texture, and the cocoa provides a rich chocolate flavor without the excess sugar. It's a satisfying treat for those on a ketogenic diet.

Almond Flour Chocolate Chip Cookies

Ingredients:

- 2 cups almond flour
- 1/2 cup unsalted butter, softened
- 1/3 cup keto-friendly sweetener (e.g., erythritol or monk fruit)
- 1 large egg
- 1 teaspoon vanilla extract
- 1/2 teaspoon baking soda
- 1/4 teaspoon salt
- 1/2 cup sugar-free chocolate chips

Instructions:

Preheat the Oven:
- Preheat your oven to 350°F (175°C). Line a baking sheet with parchment paper.

Combine Dry Ingredients:
- In a bowl, whisk together the almond flour, baking soda, and salt. Set aside.

Cream Butter and Sweetener:
- In a separate large bowl, cream together the softened butter and keto-friendly sweetener until light and fluffy.

Add Egg and Vanilla:
- Beat in the egg and vanilla extract until well combined.

Combine Wet and Dry Mixtures:
- Gradually add the almond flour mixture to the wet ingredients, mixing until a cookie dough forms.

Fold in Chocolate Chips:
- Gently fold in the sugar-free chocolate chips until evenly distributed throughout the dough.

Scoop Dough onto Baking Sheet:
- Using a cookie scoop or spoon, drop rounded tablespoons of cookie dough onto the prepared baking sheet, spacing them about 2 inches apart.

Flatten Cookies (Optional):
- If you prefer flatter cookies, lightly flatten each dough ball with the back of a spoon or your fingers.

Bake:
- Bake in the preheated oven for 10-12 minutes or until the edges are golden brown. Keep an eye on them to prevent over-baking.

Cool:
- Allow the cookies to cool on the baking sheet for a few minutes before transferring them to a wire rack to cool completely.

Enjoy:
- Once cooled, enjoy your delicious Almond Flour Chocolate Chip Cookies!

These cookies are not only keto-friendly but also gluten-free and low in carbs. The almond flour provides a nutty flavor and a tender texture, while the sugar-free chocolate chips add the perfect touch of sweetness. It's a delightful treat for those following a ketogenic diet.

Keto Cheesecake Bites

Ingredients:

For the Crust:

- 1 cup almond flour
- 3 tablespoons melted butter
- 1 tablespoon powdered erythritol (or your preferred keto-friendly sweetener)
- 1/2 teaspoon vanilla extract
- A pinch of salt

For the Cheesecake Filling:

- 8 ounces cream cheese, softened
- 1/3 cup powdered erythritol
- 1 large egg
- 1 teaspoon vanilla extract
- Zest of 1 lemon (optional)

Instructions:

1. Preheat the Oven:

- Preheat your oven to 325°F (163°C) and line a mini muffin tin with paper liners.

2. Make the Crust:

- In a bowl, combine almond flour, melted butter, powdered erythritol, vanilla extract, and a pinch of salt. Mix until well combined.

3. Form Crust in Muffin Tin:

- Spoon about a tablespoon of the crust mixture into each mini muffin cup. Press the mixture down to form a crust in the bottom of each cup.

4. Bake the Crust:

- Bake the crust in the preheated oven for 8-10 minutes or until it's lightly golden. Remove from the oven and let it cool while preparing the cheesecake filling.

5. Make the Cheesecake Filling:

- In a separate bowl, beat the softened cream cheese until smooth.
- Add powdered erythritol, egg, vanilla extract, and lemon zest (if using). Beat until well combined and smooth.

6. Fill the Muffin Cups:

- Spoon the cheesecake filling over the cooled crusts in the mini muffin tin.

7. Bake the Cheesecake Bites:

- Bake in the preheated oven for 15-18 minutes or until the edges are set, and the centers are slightly jiggly.

8. Cool and Chill:

- Allow the cheesecake bites to cool in the muffin tin, then transfer them to the refrigerator to chill for at least 2 hours or until fully set.

9. Serve:

- Once chilled, remove the cheesecake bites from the muffin tin. Optionally, you can top them with a small dollop of whipped cream or a sprinkle of grated lemon zest.

10. Enjoy:

- Enjoy these delightful Keto Cheesecake Bites as a satisfying low-carb treat!

These Keto Cheesecake Bites are rich, creamy, and perfectly portioned for a keto-friendly dessert. The almond flour crust adds a nice crunch, while the cheesecake filling is smooth and satisfying. They are a great option for satisfying your sweet tooth while staying within your keto dietary goals.

Coconut Flour Lemon Poppy Seed Muffins

Ingredients:

- 1/2 cup coconut flour
- 1/4 cup almond flour
- 1/3 cup erythritol or your preferred keto-friendly sweetener
- 1 teaspoon baking powder
- 1/4 teaspoon salt
- 1/4 cup unsalted butter, melted
- 4 large eggs
- 1/4 cup coconut milk or almond milk
- Zest of 1 lemon
- 2 tablespoons fresh lemon juice
- 1 teaspoon vanilla extract
- 1 tablespoon poppy seeds

Instructions:

Preheat the Oven:
- Preheat your oven to 350°F (175°C).

Prepare Muffin Cups:
- Line a muffin tin with paper liners or grease the cups well.

Combine Dry Ingredients:
- In a bowl, whisk together coconut flour, almond flour, erythritol, baking powder, and salt.

Mix Wet Ingredients:
- In a separate bowl, whisk together melted butter, eggs, coconut milk, lemon zest, lemon juice, and vanilla extract.

Combine Wet and Dry Mixtures:
- Add the wet ingredients to the dry ingredients and mix until well combined.

Add Poppy Seeds:
- Gently fold in the poppy seeds into the batter.

Let the Batter Rest:
- Allow the batter to rest for a few minutes to let the coconut flour absorb the liquids. Coconut flour tends to absorb moisture, and this short resting time will give you a better consistency.

Fill Muffin Cups:

- Spoon the batter into the prepared muffin cups, filling each about two-thirds full.

Bake:
- Bake in the preheated oven for 20-25 minutes or until a toothpick inserted into the center comes out clean.

Cool:
- Allow the muffins to cool in the tin for a few minutes before transferring them to a wire rack to cool completely.

Serve:
- Serve these Coconut Flour Lemon Poppy Seed Muffins as a delightful keto-friendly treat!

These muffins offer a burst of citrusy flavor from the lemon zest and juice, complemented by the nutty richness of almond flour and the subtle sweetness of erythritol. They're a perfect keto-friendly option for a quick breakfast or a snack.

Avocado Chocolate Mousse

Ingredients:

- 2 ripe avocados, peeled and pitted
- 1/4 cup unsweetened cocoa powder
- 1/4 cup almond milk or coconut milk (unsweetened)
- 1/4 cup maple syrup or keto-friendly sweetener (adjust to taste)
- 1 teaspoon vanilla extract
- A pinch of salt
- Optional toppings: whipped cream, berries, or chopped nuts

Instructions:

Prepare the Avocados:
- Scoop out the flesh from the ripe avocados and place them in a blender or food processor.

Add Cocoa Powder:
- Add the unsweetened cocoa powder to the blender.

Pour in Almond Milk:
- Add the almond milk (or coconut milk) to the blender.

Sweeten It Up:
- Pour in the maple syrup (or your preferred sweetener) to the mixture.

Add Flavor:
- Add the vanilla extract and a pinch of salt for flavor balance.

Blend Until Smooth:
- Blend all the ingredients until you achieve a smooth and creamy consistency. You may need to stop and scrape down the sides of the blender to ensure everything is well incorporated.

Taste and Adjust:
- Taste the mousse and adjust the sweetness or cocoa level according to your preference.

Chill:
- Transfer the Avocado Chocolate Mousse to serving bowls or jars.
- Refrigerate for at least 1-2 hours to allow the mousse to chill and thicken.

Serve:
- Once chilled, you can serve the Avocado Chocolate Mousse on its own or with optional toppings like whipped cream, berries, or chopped nuts.

Enjoy:

- Enjoy this creamy and nutritious Avocado Chocolate Mousse as a guilt-free dessert.

This Avocado Chocolate Mousse is not only a delicious treat but also a healthier alternative to traditional chocolate mousse. The avocados provide a creamy texture while adding healthy fats and nutrients to the dessert. It's suitable for various dietary preferences, including keto and vegan.

Keto Chocolate Fat Bombs

Ingredients:

- 1/2 cup coconut oil, melted
- 1/4 cup unsweetened cocoa powder
- 1/4 cup almond butter or peanut butter (unsweetened)
- 2 tablespoons powdered erythritol or your preferred keto-friendly sweetener
- 1/2 teaspoon vanilla extract
- A pinch of salt

Optional Add-Ins:

- Chopped nuts (almonds, walnuts, or pecans)
- Unsweetened shredded coconut
- Chia seeds

Instructions:

Melt Coconut Oil:
- In a heatproof bowl, melt the coconut oil until it's in a liquid state.

Add Cocoa Powder:
- Add the unsweetened cocoa powder to the melted coconut oil. Stir until well combined.

Sweeten and Flavor:
- Mix in the powdered erythritol, almond butter (or peanut butter), vanilla extract, and a pinch of salt. Stir until smooth.

Optional Add-Ins:
- If desired, add chopped nuts, shredded coconut, or chia seeds for extra texture and flavor. Mix well.

Mold the Fat Bombs:
- Spoon the mixture into silicone molds or use a small ice cube tray. Ensure each section is filled evenly.

Freeze:
- Place the molds in the freezer for at least 1-2 hours or until the fat bombs are firm and set.

Remove from Molds:

- Once frozen, pop the fat bombs out of the molds and transfer them to an airtight container.

Store:
- Store the Keto Chocolate Fat Bombs in the freezer for a quick and satisfying treat.

Enjoy:
- Enjoy these fat bombs as a delicious and keto-friendly snack or dessert.

These Keto Chocolate Fat Bombs are a tasty way to increase your healthy fat intake while keeping carbs low. They're convenient for those following a ketogenic diet and can be customized with various add-ins to suit your preferences. Make a batch and keep them in the freezer for a quick energy boost whenever needed.

Sugar-Free Vanilla Ice Cream

Ingredients:

- 2 cups heavy cream
- 1 cup unsweetened almond milk or coconut milk
- 1/2 cup powdered erythritol or your preferred sugar substitute
- 1 tablespoon pure vanilla extract
- 4 large egg yolks
- A pinch of salt

Instructions:

Prepare an Ice Cream Maker:
- If you have an ice cream maker, ensure that the bowl is properly frozen according to the manufacturer's instructions.

Combine Cream and Milk:
- In a saucepan, combine the heavy cream and almond milk (or coconut milk). Heat the mixture over medium heat until it just starts to simmer. Do not bring it to a boil.

Whisk in Sweetener:
- In a separate bowl, whisk together the powdered erythritol and egg yolks until well combined.

Temper the Eggs:
- Slowly pour a small amount of the hot cream mixture into the egg mixture while whisking constantly. This helps temper the eggs, preventing them from curdling.

Combine Mixtures:
- Gradually add the egg mixture back into the saucepan with the remaining cream mixture, whisking continuously.

Cook Custard Base:
- Cook the custard over medium heat, stirring constantly, until it thickens enough to coat the back of a spoon. Do not let it boil.

Add Vanilla Extract:
- Remove the saucepan from heat and stir in the vanilla extract.

Strain (Optional):
- For a smoother texture, you can strain the custard through a fine-mesh sieve to remove any cooked egg bits.

Chill Custard:

- Allow the custard to cool to room temperature and then refrigerate it for at least 4 hours or overnight until thoroughly chilled.

Churn Ice Cream:
- Once chilled, churn the custard in your ice cream maker according to the manufacturer's instructions.

Transfer and Freeze:
- Transfer the churned ice cream to a lidded container and freeze for an additional 2-4 hours or until firm.

Serve:
- Scoop and serve the Sugar-Free Vanilla Ice Cream on its own or with your favorite toppings.

This Sugar-Free Vanilla Ice Cream provides a creamy and satisfying dessert without the added sugars. Adjust the sweetness to your liking and enjoy a guilt-free frozen treat.

Chocolate Peanut Butter Keto Cups

Ingredients:

For the Chocolate Layer:

- 1/2 cup coconut oil, melted
- 1/4 cup unsweetened cocoa powder
- 2 tablespoons powdered erythritol or your preferred keto-friendly sweetener
- 1/2 teaspoon vanilla extract
- A pinch of salt

For the Peanut Butter Filling:

- 1/4 cup sugar-free peanut butter
- 2 tablespoons powdered erythritol
- 1 tablespoon coconut flour (optional, for added texture)

Instructions:

1. Prepare the Chocolate Layer:

1.1. In a bowl, combine melted coconut oil, unsweetened cocoa powder, powdered erythritol, vanilla extract, and a pinch of salt. Mix until smooth.

1.2. Line a mini muffin tin with paper liners or use silicone molds.

1.3. Spoon a small amount of the chocolate mixture into the bottom of each cup, covering the base. Reserve some chocolate for the top layer.

1.4. Place the muffin tin in the freezer to set the chocolate layer while you prepare the peanut butter filling.

2. Make the Peanut Butter Filling:

2.1. In a separate bowl, mix together sugar-free peanut butter, powdered erythritol, and coconut flour (if using) until well combined.

2.2. Remove the muffin tin from the freezer and place a small amount of the peanut butter mixture on top of the chocolate layer in each cup.

2.3. Press down the peanut butter layer gently to flatten.

3. Add the Top Chocolate Layer:

3.1. Use the remaining chocolate mixture to cover the peanut butter filling in each cup.

3.2. Smooth the top layer with a spatula or back of a spoon.

4. Freeze:

4.1. Place the muffin tin back in the freezer and let the chocolate peanut butter cups set for at least 1-2 hours, or until completely firm.

5. Enjoy:

5.1. Once frozen, remove the cups from the muffin tin and store them in an airtight container in the freezer.

5.2. Enjoy these delicious Chocolate Peanut Butter Keto Cups straight from the freezer whenever you crave a sweet and satisfying keto-friendly treat!

These chocolate peanut butter cups are not only keto-friendly but also a great way to curb your sweet cravings without the added sugar. Adjust the sweetness to your liking and experiment with different nut butters for variety.

Keto Pumpkin Pie Bars

Ingredients:

For the Crust:

- 1 1/2 cups almond flour
- 1/4 cup coconut flour
- 1/4 cup powdered erythritol
- 1/2 cup unsalted butter, melted

For the Pumpkin Filling:

- 1 cup canned pumpkin puree
- 1/2 cup heavy cream
- 2 large eggs
- 1/2 cup powdered erythritol
- 1 teaspoon vanilla extract
- 1 teaspoon pumpkin spice blend (cinnamon, nutmeg, ginger, and cloves)

Instructions:

1. Preheat the Oven:

Preheat your oven to 350°F (175°C). Line a square baking dish (8x8 inches) with parchment paper, leaving some overhang for easy removal.

2. Make the Crust:

In a mixing bowl, combine almond flour, coconut flour, powdered erythritol, and melted butter. Stir until well combined. Press the mixture into the bottom of the prepared baking dish to form an even crust.

3. Bake the Crust:

Bake the crust in the preheated oven for 10-12 minutes or until it's golden brown. Remove from the oven and let it cool while you prepare the filling.

4. Prepare the Pumpkin Filling:

In a separate bowl, whisk together pumpkin puree, heavy cream, eggs, powdered erythritol, vanilla extract, and pumpkin spice blend until smooth and well combined.

5. Assemble and Bake:

Pour the pumpkin filling over the cooled crust, spreading it evenly. Bake in the oven for 25-30 minutes or until the center is set.

6. Cool and Refrigerate:

Allow the pumpkin pie bars to cool in the baking dish. Once cooled, refrigerate for at least 2-3 hours or overnight to set.

7. Serve:

Once fully chilled, use the parchment paper overhang to lift the bars out of the baking dish. Cut into squares and serve. Optionally, top with whipped cream or a sprinkle of cinnamon before serving.

These Keto Pumpkin Pie Bars offer a delicious low-carb alternative to traditional pumpkin pie, making them a perfect treat for those following a keto lifestyle. Enjoy!

Almond Butter Keto Brownies

Ingredients:

Dry Ingredients:

- 1 cup almond flour
- 1/3 cup unsweetened cocoa powder
- 1/2 teaspoon baking powder
- 1/4 teaspoon salt

Wet Ingredients:

- 1 cup almond butter (unsweetened)
- 1/2 cup unsalted butter, melted
- 3/4 cup powdered erythritol or your preferred low-carb sweetener
- 3 large eggs
- 1 teaspoon vanilla extract

Optional Add-ins:

- 1/2 cup sugar-free chocolate chips or chopped dark chocolate

Instructions:

1. Preheat the Oven:

Preheat your oven to 350°F (175°C). Grease or line an 8x8-inch baking dish with parchment paper.

2. Mix Dry Ingredients:

In a medium-sized bowl, whisk together the almond flour, cocoa powder, baking powder, and salt. Ensure there are no lumps.

3. Combine Wet Ingredients:

In a separate large bowl, combine the almond butter, melted butter, powdered erythritol, eggs, and vanilla extract. Mix until well combined and smooth.

4. Combine Wet and Dry Mixtures:

Add the dry ingredients to the wet ingredients and stir until just combined. Be careful not to overmix. If desired, fold in sugar-free chocolate chips or chopped dark chocolate.

5. Transfer to Baking Dish:

Pour the brownie batter into the prepared baking dish and spread it evenly.

6. Bake:

Bake in the preheated oven for 20-25 minutes or until the edges are set, and a toothpick inserted into the center comes out with a few moist crumbs (not wet batter).

7. Cool and Cut:

Allow the brownies to cool completely in the baking dish. Once cooled, lift them out using the parchment paper overhang and cut into squares.

8. Serve:

Serve the almond butter keto brownies and enjoy! Optionally, you can dust them with cocoa powder or a sprinkle of powdered erythritol before serving.

These brownies are rich, fudgy, and low in carbs, making them a delicious treat for those following a keto diet.

Keto Chocolate Covered Strawberries

Ingredients:

- 1 cup sugar-free chocolate chips or dark chocolate (at least 70% cocoa)
- 1 tablespoon coconut oil (optional, for smoother chocolate)
- 1 pint fresh strawberries, washed and dried

Optional Toppings:

- Crushed nuts (e.g., almonds, pecans)
- Shredded coconut
- Chopped mint leaves

Instructions:

1. Prepare the Strawberries:

Wash and thoroughly dry the strawberries. Make sure they are completely dry, as any moisture can cause the chocolate to seize.

2. Melt the Chocolate:

In a heatproof bowl, melt the sugar-free chocolate chips or dark chocolate. You can use a microwave (in 20-second intervals, stirring between each) or a double boiler. If using a microwave, be cautious not to overheat the chocolate.

Optional: Add coconut oil to the melted chocolate for a smoother consistency.

3. Dip the Strawberries:

Hold each strawberry by the stem and dip it into the melted chocolate, swirling to coat evenly. Allow any excess chocolate to drip off.

4. Optional Toppings:

If desired, roll the chocolate-covered strawberries in crushed nuts, shredded coconut, or chopped mint leaves while the chocolate is still wet.

5. Set on Parchment Paper:

Place the chocolate-covered strawberries on a parchment paper-lined tray or plate, ensuring they are not touching each other.

6. Chill:

Place the tray of chocolate-covered strawberries in the refrigerator for at least 30 minutes to allow the chocolate to set.

7. Serve:

Once the chocolate is firm, you can transfer the keto chocolate-covered strawberries to a serving plate. Enjoy them as a delightful and low-carb dessert!

These keto chocolate-covered strawberries make for a delicious and elegant treat, perfect for special occasions or as a sweet indulgence on a low-carb diet.

No-Bake Coconut Almond Energy Balls

Ingredients:

- 1 cup old-fashioned rolled oats
- 1/2 cup shredded coconut (unsweetened)
- 1/2 cup almond butter
- 1/3 cup honey or maple syrup
- 1/2 cup chopped almonds
- 1 teaspoon vanilla extract
- A pinch of salt (optional)

Instructions:

In a large bowl, combine the rolled oats, shredded coconut, chopped almonds, and a pinch of salt (if using).

In a small saucepan, heat the almond butter and honey (or maple syrup) over low heat, stirring until well combined. Remove from heat and stir in the vanilla extract.

Pour the almond butter mixture over the dry ingredients in the bowl. Mix well until everything is evenly combined.

Allow the mixture to cool slightly, as it will be easier to handle. Once it's cool enough to touch, use your hands to roll the mixture into bite-sized balls. If the mixture is too sticky, you can wet your hands slightly.

Place the energy balls on a plate or tray and refrigerate for at least 30 minutes to firm up.

Once the energy balls have set, transfer them to an airtight container and store them in the refrigerator. They can be kept for up to two weeks, though they're likely to be enjoyed before then!

Feel free to customize this recipe by adding ingredients like chia seeds, flaxseeds, or chocolate chips. Enjoy your no-bake coconut almond energy balls as a quick and nutritious snack!

Keto Chocolate Mug Cake

Ingredients:

- 2 tablespoons almond flour
- 1 tablespoon cocoa powder (unsweetened)
- 1 tablespoon powdered erythritol or your preferred keto-friendly sweetener
- 1/4 teaspoon baking powder
- A pinch of salt
- 2 tablespoons unsweetened almond milk
- 1 tablespoon melted butter
- 1/4 teaspoon vanilla extract
- 1 large egg

Instructions:

In a microwave-safe mug, whisk together the almond flour, cocoa powder, erythritol, baking powder, and a pinch of salt.
Add the almond milk, melted butter, vanilla extract, and egg to the dry ingredients. Mix well until the batter is smooth and well combined.
Microwave the mug on high for 1.5 to 2 minutes, depending on the wattage of your microwave. Keep an eye on it to prevent overflowing. The cake should rise and firm up.
Allow the mug cake to cool for a minute or two before digging in.
Optionally, you can top it with whipped cream, a dollop of keto-friendly ice cream, or a sprinkle of chopped nuts.

Enjoy your quick and delicious Keto Chocolate Mug Cake! It's a satisfying treat without the guilt of added sugars and excess carbs.

Raspberry Almond Chia Pudding

Ingredients:

- 1/4 cup chia seeds
- 1 cup almond milk (unsweetened)
- 1/2 teaspoon almond extract
- 1-2 tablespoons keto-friendly sweetener (e.g., erythritol or stevia), adjust to taste
- 1/2 cup fresh raspberries
- Sliced almonds for topping (optional)

Instructions:

In a bowl, mix together chia seeds, almond milk, almond extract, and your chosen keto-friendly sweetener. Stir well to combine.
Let the mixture sit for about 5 minutes, then stir again to prevent clumping.
Repeat this process a couple of times over the next 15-20 minutes until the chia seeds begin to absorb the liquid and thicken the mixture.
Once the chia pudding has reached a thick consistency, cover the bowl and refrigerate it for at least 2-3 hours, or overnight. This allows the chia seeds to fully absorb the liquid.
Before serving, give the pudding a good stir to ensure it's well mixed and smooth.
In serving glasses or bowls, layer the chia pudding with fresh raspberries.
Optionally, top the pudding with sliced almonds for added texture and flavor.

Enjoy your Raspberry Almond Chia Pudding as a tasty and satisfying keto-friendly dessert or breakfast. Feel free to customize it with other low-carb berries or nuts according to your preferences!

Keto Almond Joy Fat Bombs

Ingredients:

- 1 cup shredded coconut (unsweetened)
- 1/2 cup coconut oil (unrefined, melted)
- 1/4 cup almond butter
- 2 tablespoons unsweetened cocoa powder
- 1-2 tablespoons powdered erythritol or another keto-friendly sweetener (adjust to taste)
- 1/2 teaspoon almond extract
- Almonds (whole or sliced), for topping

Instructions:

In a bowl, combine the shredded coconut, melted coconut oil, almond butter, cocoa powder, powdered sweetener, and almond extract. Mix well until all ingredients are fully combined.
Taste the mixture and adjust the sweetness if needed by adding more sweetener.
Line a mini muffin tin with paper or silicone liners.
Spoon the mixture evenly into the muffin tin, filling each cup about halfway.
Press an almond (or a few almond slices) into the center of each fat bomb.
Place the muffin tin in the freezer and let the fat bombs set for at least 1-2 hours, or until they are firm.
Once the fat bombs are set, remove them from the freezer. If you used paper liners, they should easily peel away.
Store the Almond Joy Fat Bombs in an airtight container in the freezer. They can be enjoyed straight from the freezer.

These Keto Almond Joy Fat Bombs are a satisfying and flavorful treat, rich in healthy fats. Enjoy them as a quick snack or dessert while following a ketogenic diet.

Blueberry Coconut Flour Mug Cake

Ingredients:

- 3 tablespoons coconut flour
- 1/4 teaspoon baking powder
- A pinch of salt
- 2 tablespoons keto-friendly sweetener (e.g., erythritol or stevia)
- 2 tablespoons coconut oil, melted
- 1/4 cup unsweetened almond milk
- 1/2 teaspoon vanilla extract
- 1 large egg
- 1/4 cup fresh or frozen blueberries

Instructions:

In a microwave-safe mug, whisk together the coconut flour, baking powder, salt, and sweetener until well combined.
Add the melted coconut oil, almond milk, vanilla extract, and egg to the dry ingredients. Mix well until a smooth batter forms.
Gently fold in the blueberries into the batter.
Microwave the mug on high for 2-3 minutes, depending on the wattage of your microwave. Keep an eye on it to prevent overflowing. The cake should rise and firm up.
Allow the mug cake to cool for a minute or two before digging in.
Optionally, you can top it with a dollop of whipped cream or a drizzle of sugar-free syrup.

Enjoy your Blueberry Coconut Flour Mug Cake as a quick and delicious keto-friendly dessert!

Keto Chocolate Hazelnut Truffles

Ingredients:

- 1 cup roasted hazelnuts
- 1/4 cup unsweetened cocoa powder
- 1/4 cup powdered erythritol or another keto-friendly sweetener
- 2 tablespoons coconut oil, melted
- 1 teaspoon vanilla extract
- A pinch of salt
- 3 oz (85g) dark chocolate (at least 70% cocoa), chopped (for coating)

Instructions:

Prepare Hazelnuts:
- If your hazelnuts are not already roasted, you can roast them by placing them on a baking sheet in a preheated oven at 350°F (175°C) for about 10-12 minutes. Once roasted, rub the hazelnuts in a clean kitchen towel to remove the skins.

Make Hazelnut Butter:
- In a food processor, blend the roasted hazelnuts until they turn into a smooth hazelnut butter. This may take a few minutes, and you might need to scrape down the sides of the processor occasionally.

Prepare Truffle Mixture:
- In a bowl, combine the hazelnut butter, cocoa powder, powdered sweetener, melted coconut oil, vanilla extract, and a pinch of salt. Mix until you have a smooth and well-incorporated mixture.

Chill the Mixture:
- Place the mixture in the refrigerator for about 30 minutes to an hour until it's firm enough to handle.

Shape Truffles:
- Once the mixture is firm, use your hands to roll it into small truffle-sized balls and place them on a parchment paper-lined tray.

Coat with Chocolate:
- Melt the dark chocolate using a double boiler or in short bursts in the microwave. Dip each truffle into the melted chocolate, coating it evenly. Use a fork to lift the truffle out of the chocolate, letting any excess drip off.

Chill Again:

- Place the coated truffles back on the parchment paper and refrigerate until the chocolate coating sets.

Serve and Enjoy:
- Once the chocolate has hardened, your Keto Chocolate Hazelnut Truffles are ready to be enjoyed. Keep them stored in the refrigerator.

These truffles offer a delightful combination of chocolate and hazelnut flavors without the excess carbs, making them a perfect keto-friendly treat.

Lemon Cheesecake Fat Bombs

Ingredients:

- 8 oz (225g) cream cheese, softened
- 1/4 cup unsalted butter, softened
- 1/4 cup coconut oil, melted
- 1/4 cup powdered erythritol or another keto-friendly sweetener
- Zest of 1 lemon
- 2 tablespoons fresh lemon juice
- 1/2 teaspoon vanilla extract
- A pinch of salt

Instructions:

Prepare Ingredients:
- Make sure the cream cheese and butter are softened at room temperature.

Mix Ingredients:
- In a mixing bowl, combine the softened cream cheese, softened butter, melted coconut oil, powdered sweetener, lemon zest, fresh lemon juice, vanilla extract, and a pinch of salt.

Blend Until Smooth:
- Use a hand mixer or a stand mixer to blend the ingredients until smooth and well combined. You want a creamy consistency with no lumps.

Chill the Mixture:
- Place the mixture in the refrigerator for about 30 minutes to an hour until it's firm enough to handle.

Shape into Balls:
- Once the mixture has chilled, use your hands to roll it into small, bite-sized balls or fat bomb shapes.

Optional Coating:
- If desired, you can roll the fat bombs in additional lemon zest or unsweetened shredded coconut for extra flavor and texture.

Chill Again:
- Place the shaped fat bombs on a tray lined with parchment paper and refrigerate until they firm up.

Serve and Enjoy:

- Once the Lemon Cheesecake Fat Bombs have set, they are ready to be enjoyed. Keep them stored in the refrigerator.

These fat bombs provide a satisfying and refreshing burst of lemony flavor while offering a dose of healthy fats for those following a ketogenic diet. Enjoy them as a snack or dessert!

Chocolate Avocado Keto Ice Cream

Ingredients:

- 2 ripe avocados, peeled and pitted
- 1/2 cup unsweetened cocoa powder
- 1/2 cup coconut milk (full-fat)
- 1/2 cup almond milk
- 1/3 cup powdered erythritol or your preferred keto-friendly sweetener (adjust to taste)
- 1 teaspoon vanilla extract
- A pinch of salt

Instructions:

Blend Avocados:
- In a blender or food processor, combine the ripe avocados, cocoa powder, coconut milk, almond milk, powdered sweetener, vanilla extract, and a pinch of salt.

Blend until Smooth:
- Blend the ingredients until the mixture is smooth and well combined. You may need to stop and scrape down the sides of the blender or food processor to ensure everything is incorporated.

Taste and Adjust:
- Taste the mixture and adjust the sweetness if needed by adding more sweetener.

Chill the Mixture:
- Transfer the mixture to a bowl and refrigerate for at least 2-3 hours, or until well chilled. This step helps improve the texture of the ice cream.

Churn the Ice Cream:
- If you have an ice cream maker, churn the chilled mixture according to the manufacturer's instructions until it reaches a soft-serve consistency.
- If you don't have an ice cream maker, you can pour the chilled mixture into a shallow dish and place it in the freezer. Every 30 minutes, stir the mixture with a fork to break up ice crystals until it reaches your desired consistency.

Serve or Freeze:

- Once the ice cream has reached your desired consistency, you can serve it immediately or transfer it to an airtight container and freeze for a firmer texture.

Enjoy:
- Scoop the Chocolate Avocado Keto Ice Cream into bowls or cones and enjoy your delicious and creamy keto-friendly treat!

This chocolate avocado ice cream is rich, creamy, and satisfying, making it a perfect low-carb dessert option.

Keto Peanut Butter Cookies

Ingredients:

- 1 cup peanut butter (unsweetened)
- 1/2 cup almond flour
- 1/2 cup erythritol or another keto-friendly sweetener
- 1 large egg
- 1 teaspoon vanilla extract
- 1/2 teaspoon baking soda
- A pinch of salt

Instructions:

Preheat Oven:
- Preheat your oven to 350°F (175°C) and line a baking sheet with parchment paper.

Combine Ingredients:
- In a mixing bowl, combine the peanut butter, almond flour, erythritol, egg, vanilla extract, baking soda, and a pinch of salt. Mix well until all ingredients are thoroughly combined.

Form Dough Balls:
- Take small portions of the dough and roll them into balls. Place the balls on the prepared baking sheet, leaving enough space between each cookie.

Flatten with a Fork:
- Use a fork to gently flatten each cookie and create a crisscross pattern on the top.

Bake:
- Bake in the preheated oven for about 10-12 minutes or until the edges are golden brown. Keep an eye on them to avoid over-baking, as almond flour can brown quickly.

Cool:
- Allow the cookies to cool on the baking sheet for a few minutes before transferring them to a wire rack to cool completely.

Enjoy:
- Once cooled, your Keto Peanut Butter Cookies are ready to be enjoyed! Store them in an airtight container at room temperature.

These cookies are rich in peanut butter flavor and provide a satisfying sweet treat without the excess carbs. Feel free to customize by adding sugar-free chocolate chips or chopped nuts if desired.

Pumpkin Spice Keto Fat Bombs

Ingredients:

- 1/2 cup canned pumpkin puree
- 1/2 cup coconut oil, melted
- 1/4 cup unsweetened almond butter
- 2 tablespoons powdered erythritol or another keto-friendly sweetener
- 1 teaspoon pumpkin spice blend (or a mix of cinnamon, nutmeg, ginger, and cloves)
- A pinch of salt

Instructions:

Mix Ingredients:
- In a bowl, combine the pumpkin puree, melted coconut oil, almond butter, powdered sweetener, pumpkin spice blend, and a pinch of salt. Mix well until all ingredients are thoroughly combined.

Taste and Adjust:
- Taste the mixture and adjust the sweetness or spice levels to your liking by adding more sweetener or spice if needed.

Shape Fat Bombs:
- Spoon the mixture into silicone molds or shape them into small balls using your hands. If you use molds, make sure they are freezer-safe.

Freeze:
- Place the fat bombs in the freezer for at least 2-3 hours or until they are firm.

Serve:
- Once the fat bombs are set, remove them from the molds or simply pop them out of your silicone molds. They are ready to be enjoyed!

Store:
- Store the Pumpkin Spice Keto Fat Bombs in an airtight container in the freezer. They can be enjoyed straight from the freezer whenever you need a tasty and satisfying low-carb treat.

These fat bombs are not only delicious but also provide a dose of healthy fats, making them a great addition to a ketogenic lifestyle. Enjoy the flavors of pumpkin spice without the extra carbs!

Coconut Flour Chocolate Zucchini Bread

Ingredients:

- 1 cup shredded zucchini (excess water squeezed out)
- 4 large eggs
- 1/4 cup coconut oil, melted
- 1/2 cup coconut flour
- 1/4 cup unsweetened cocoa powder
- 1/2 cup powdered erythritol or another keto-friendly sweetener
- 1 teaspoon baking powder
- 1/2 teaspoon vanilla extract
- A pinch of salt
- 1/3 cup sugar-free chocolate chips (optional)

Instructions:

Preheat Oven:
- Preheat your oven to 350°F (175°C). Grease or line a loaf pan with parchment paper.

Prepare Zucchini:
- Shred the zucchini using a grater and squeeze out the excess water. Set aside.

Mix Wet Ingredients:
- In a large bowl, whisk together the eggs, melted coconut oil, and vanilla extract until well combined.

Combine Dry Ingredients:
- In a separate bowl, combine the coconut flour, cocoa powder, powdered sweetener, baking powder, and a pinch of salt.

Combine Wet and Dry Ingredients:
- Add the dry ingredients to the wet ingredients and mix until well combined. The batter will be thick.

Add Zucchini and Chocolate Chips:
- Fold in the shredded zucchini until evenly distributed throughout the batter. If desired, fold in sugar-free chocolate chips.

Transfer to Pan:
- Transfer the batter to the prepared loaf pan, spreading it out evenly.

Bake:
- Bake in the preheated oven for 40-50 minutes or until a toothpick inserted into the center comes out clean.

Cool:
- Allow the Coconut Flour Chocolate Zucchini Bread to cool in the pan for 10-15 minutes, then transfer it to a wire rack to cool completely.

Slice and Serve:
- Once cooled, slice and serve. Enjoy your low-carb and keto-friendly chocolate zucchini bread!

This moist and chocolatey bread is a delightful way to incorporate zucchini into your diet while satisfying your sweet cravings on a keto or low-carb lifestyle.

Keto Chocolate Almond Bark

Ingredients:

- 1 cup sugar-free dark chocolate (at least 70% cocoa)
- 1/2 cup almonds, chopped
- 1 tablespoon coconut oil (optional, for smoother consistency)
- A pinch of sea salt (optional)

Instructions:

Prepare a Baking Sheet:
- Line a baking sheet with parchment paper or a silicone baking mat.

Melt Chocolate:
- In a microwave-safe bowl or using a double boiler, melt the sugar-free dark chocolate. If using the microwave, heat in 20-30 second intervals, stirring between each interval until fully melted. If desired, add coconut oil to the chocolate for a smoother consistency.

Add Almonds:
- Stir in the chopped almonds into the melted chocolate, making sure they are well-coated.

Spread on Baking Sheet:
- Pour the chocolate and almond mixture onto the prepared baking sheet. Use a spatula to spread it evenly to your desired thickness.

Optional: Add Sea Salt:
- Sprinkle a pinch of sea salt over the chocolate if you like the combination of sweet and salty flavors.

Chill:
- Place the baking sheet in the refrigerator or freezer to let the chocolate set. This will take about 1-2 hours.

Break into Pieces:
- Once the chocolate is fully set, remove it from the refrigerator or freezer. Use your hands or a knife to break it into bark-like pieces.

Store:
- Store the Keto Chocolate Almond Bark in an airtight container in the refrigerator. It can also be stored in the freezer for a longer shelf life.

Enjoy:
- Enjoy your Keto Chocolate Almond Bark as a delicious, low-carb, and satisfying treat!

Feel free to customize this recipe by adding other keto-friendly ingredients like shredded coconut, chopped nuts, or a dash of your favorite sugar-free sweetener.

Vanilla Coconut Flour Mug Cake

Ingredients:

- 3 tablespoons coconut flour
- 1/4 teaspoon baking powder
- A pinch of salt
- 2 tablespoons unsalted butter, melted
- 2 tablespoons unsweetened almond milk
- 1 large egg
- 1/2 teaspoon vanilla extract
- Keto-friendly sweetener to taste (e.g., erythritol or stevia)

Instructions:

Prepare Mug:
- Grease a microwave-safe mug with a little butter or cooking spray.

Mix Dry Ingredients:
- In a small bowl, whisk together the coconut flour, baking powder, and a pinch of salt.

Combine Wet Ingredients:
- In the mug, combine the melted butter, almond milk, egg, vanilla extract, and your preferred keto-friendly sweetener. Mix well.

Add Dry Ingredients:
- Gradually add the dry ingredients to the mug, stirring continuously to avoid lumps.

Mix Thoroughly:
- Stir the mixture until it forms a smooth batter.

Microwave:
- Microwave the mug on high for 90 seconds to 2 minutes, depending on the wattage of your microwave. Keep an eye on it to prevent overflowing. The cake should rise and firm up.

Cool:
- Allow the mug cake to cool for a minute or two before eating.

Optional Toppings:
- Optionally, top the vanilla coconut flour mug cake with a dollop of whipped cream or a sprinkle of shredded coconut.

Enjoy:
- Enjoy your quick and delicious Vanilla Coconut Flour Mug Cake as a satisfying keto-friendly dessert!

Feel free to experiment with the sweetness level and adjust it according to your taste preferences. You can also add a touch of cinnamon or nutmeg for extra flavor if desired.

Keto Chocolate Chip Cookie Dough Fat Bombs

Ingredients:

- 1/2 cup almond flour
- 1/4 cup coconut flour
- 1/4 cup unsalted butter, softened
- 1/4 cup keto-friendly sweetener (e.g., erythritol or stevia)
- 1/2 teaspoon vanilla extract
- A pinch of salt
- 1/4 cup sugar-free chocolate chips

Instructions:

Mix Dry Ingredients:
- In a bowl, combine almond flour, coconut flour, and a pinch of salt. Mix well.

Cream Butter and Sweetener:
- In a separate bowl, cream together the softened butter and keto-friendly sweetener until smooth.

Combine Wet and Dry Ingredients:
- Add the vanilla extract to the butter mixture and mix well. Gradually incorporate the dry ingredients into the wet ingredients, stirring until you have a cookie dough-like consistency.

Add Chocolate Chips:
- Fold in the sugar-free chocolate chips until evenly distributed throughout the dough.

Shape into Balls:
- Take small portions of the dough and roll them into bite-sized balls. Place the balls on a parchment paper-lined tray.

Chill:
- Place the tray in the refrigerator for at least 30 minutes to allow the fat bombs to firm up.

Serve:
- Once the fat bombs are set, you can serve and enjoy! Store any leftovers in an airtight container in the refrigerator.

These Keto Chocolate Chip Cookie Dough Fat Bombs are perfect for satisfying your sweet cravings while staying low-carb. Feel free to customize the recipe by adding nuts or other keto-friendly mix-ins to suit your preferences. Enjoy!

Strawberry Cheesecake Keto Fat Bombs

Ingredients:

- 4 oz (113g) cream cheese, softened
- 2 tablespoons unsalted butter, softened
- 1/2 cup fresh strawberries, hulled and diced
- 2 tablespoons powdered erythritol or another keto-friendly sweetener
- 1/2 teaspoon vanilla extract
- A pinch of salt
- 2 tablespoons coconut flour (optional, for texture)
- Additional sweetener to taste (if needed)

Instructions:

Prepare Strawberries:
- Hull and dice the fresh strawberries.

Mix Cream Cheese and Butter:
- In a mixing bowl, combine softened cream cheese and butter. Beat until well combined and smooth.

Add Sweetener and Vanilla:
- Add powdered erythritol, vanilla extract, and a pinch of salt to the cream cheese and butter mixture. Mix well.

Fold in Strawberries:
- Gently fold in the diced strawberries into the cream cheese mixture. If you prefer a smoother texture, you can use a hand mixer or blender.

Add Coconut Flour (Optional):
- If you desire a thicker consistency, add coconut flour to the mixture and combine well. Coconut flour is optional and can be omitted if you prefer a creamier texture.

Taste and Adjust Sweetness:
- Taste the mixture and adjust the sweetness if needed by adding more keto-friendly sweetener.

Shape into Balls:
- Scoop spoonfuls of the mixture and roll it into bite-sized balls.

Chill:
- Place the fat bombs in the refrigerator for at least 1-2 hours to firm up.

Serve:
- Once set, your Strawberry Cheesecake Keto Fat Bombs are ready to be enjoyed! Keep any leftovers refrigerated.

Feel free to get creative and experiment with different berries or add a touch of lemon zest for extra flavor. These fat bombs are a tasty way to boost your healthy fat intake while staying within your keto macros.

Almond Flour Keto Donuts

Ingredients:

For the Donuts:

- 2 cups almond flour
- 1/3 cup coconut flour
- 1/2 cup keto-friendly sweetener (e.g., erythritol or stevia)
- 1 teaspoon baking powder
- 1/4 teaspoon salt
- 1/2 cup unsalted butter, melted
- 3 large eggs
- 1 teaspoon vanilla extract
- 1/2 cup unsweetened almond milk

For the Glaze:

- 1/2 cup powdered erythritol or another keto-friendly powdered sweetener
- 2 tablespoons unsweetened almond milk
- 1/2 teaspoon vanilla extract
- Optional: sugar-free sprinkles or chopped nuts for topping

Instructions:

Preheat Oven:
- Preheat your oven to 350°F (175°C). Grease a donut pan with butter or cooking spray.

Mix Dry Ingredients:
- In a large bowl, whisk together almond flour, coconut flour, sweetener, baking powder, and salt.

Combine Wet Ingredients:
- In a separate bowl, mix together melted butter, eggs, vanilla extract, and almond milk.

Combine Wet and Dry Ingredients:
- Add the wet ingredients to the dry ingredients and stir until well combined. The batter should be thick.

Fill Donut Pan:
- Spoon the batter into the donut pan, filling each mold about 3/4 full.

Bake:
- Bake in the preheated oven for 15-18 minutes or until the donuts are lightly golden and a toothpick inserted into the center comes out clean.

Cool:
- Allow the donuts to cool in the pan for a few minutes, then transfer them to a wire rack to cool completely.

Make the Glaze:
- In a bowl, whisk together powdered erythritol, almond milk, and vanilla extract until you have a smooth glaze.

Dip and Top:
- Once the donuts are completely cooled, dip the tops into the glaze. Add optional toppings like sugar-free sprinkles or chopped nuts.

Set Glaze:
- Place the glazed donuts back on the wire rack to let the glaze set.

Serve and Enjoy:
- Your Almond Flour Keto Donuts are ready to be enjoyed! Store any leftovers in an airtight container.

Feel free to get creative with the glaze or add flavorings like cinnamon or nutmeg to the donut batter. These keto-friendly donuts are a delicious way to satisfy your sweet cravings without compromising your low-carb lifestyle.

Chocolate Coconut Flour Pancakes

Ingredients:

- 1/4 cup coconut flour
- 2 tablespoons unsweetened cocoa powder
- 2 tablespoons keto-friendly sweetener (e.g., erythritol or stevia)
- 1/2 teaspoon baking powder
- A pinch of salt
- 4 large eggs
- 1/4 cup unsweetened almond milk
- 2 tablespoons melted coconut oil
- 1 teaspoon vanilla extract
- Sugar-free chocolate chips (optional, for extra chocolatey goodness)
- Additional toppings like whipped cream, berries, or nuts (optional)

Instructions:

Prepare Batter:
- In a bowl, whisk together coconut flour, cocoa powder, keto-friendly sweetener, baking powder, and a pinch of salt.

Combine Wet Ingredients:
- In another bowl, whisk together eggs, almond milk, melted coconut oil, and vanilla extract.

Mix Batter:
- Add the wet ingredients to the dry ingredients and stir until well combined. Let the batter sit for a few minutes to allow the coconut flour to absorb the liquids.

Cook Pancakes:
- Heat a griddle or non-stick skillet over medium heat. Lightly grease the surface with coconut oil or butter.
- Scoop about 1/4 cup of batter onto the griddle for each pancake. If desired, sprinkle a few sugar-free chocolate chips onto each pancake.
- Cook until bubbles form on the surface, then flip and cook the other side until golden brown.

Serve:
- Remove the pancakes from the griddle and repeat until all the batter is used.

Top and Enjoy:

- Serve the chocolate coconut flour pancakes warm with your favorite toppings, such as whipped cream, berries, or nuts.

These chocolate coconut flour pancakes are not only delicious but also low in carbs, making them a perfect option for a keto-friendly breakfast or brunch. Adjust the sweetness level to your liking and get creative with toppings for a personalized touch!

Keto Chocolate Pecan Pie Bars

Ingredients:

For the Crust:

- 1 cup almond flour
- 1/4 cup coconut flour
- 1/4 cup powdered erythritol or another keto-friendly sweetener
- 1/2 cup unsalted butter, melted

For the Pecan Filling:

- 1 1/2 cups pecans, chopped
- 1/2 cup unsalted butter
- 1/2 cup powdered erythritol or another keto-friendly sweetener
- 1/3 cup heavy cream
- 1 teaspoon vanilla extract
- A pinch of salt

For the Chocolate Layer:

- 4 oz (113g) sugar-free dark chocolate, chopped
- 2 tablespoons coconut oil

Instructions:

Preheat Oven:
- Preheat your oven to 350°F (175°C). Line a square baking pan with parchment paper, leaving some overhang on the sides for easy removal.

Make the Crust:
- In a bowl, combine almond flour, coconut flour, powdered sweetener, and melted butter for the crust. Press the mixture into the bottom of the prepared pan to form an even crust.

Bake the Crust:
- Bake the crust in the preheated oven for 10-12 minutes or until it's lightly golden. Remove from the oven and let it cool slightly.

Prepare the Pecan Filling:
- In a saucepan over medium heat, combine chopped pecans, butter, powdered sweetener, heavy cream, vanilla extract, and a pinch of salt. Stir

continuously and bring the mixture to a gentle boil. Reduce the heat and simmer for 2-3 minutes until the mixture thickens slightly.

Spread Pecan Filling:
- Pour the pecan filling over the baked crust, spreading it evenly.

Bake Again:
- Return the pan to the oven and bake for an additional 15-18 minutes or until the pecan filling is set.

Make the Chocolate Layer:
- In a microwave-safe bowl, melt the sugar-free dark chocolate and coconut oil together. Stir until smooth.

Spread Chocolate Layer:
- Pour the melted chocolate over the pecan filling, spreading it evenly.

Chill and Set:
- Place the pan in the refrigerator to let the chocolate layer set. This will take at least 2 hours.

Slice and Serve:
- Once set, use the parchment paper overhang to lift the bars from the pan. Slice into squares or bars.

Enjoy:
- Your Keto Chocolate Pecan Pie Bars are ready to be enjoyed! Store any leftovers in the refrigerator.

These bars are a delightful keto-friendly dessert that captures the essence of pecan pie with a layer of rich chocolate. Enjoy the sweet and nutty flavors without the excess carbs!

Lemon Almond Flour Shortbread Cookies

Ingredients:

- 1 cup almond flour
- 1/4 cup coconut flour
- 1/3 cup powdered erythritol or another keto-friendly sweetener
- Zest of 1 lemon
- 1/2 cup unsalted butter, softened
- 1 teaspoon vanilla extract
- A pinch of salt

Instructions:

Preheat Oven:
- Preheat your oven to 325°F (163°C). Line a baking sheet with parchment paper.

Mix Dry Ingredients:
- In a bowl, whisk together almond flour, coconut flour, powdered sweetener, and a pinch of salt.

Add Lemon Zest:
- Add the lemon zest to the dry ingredients and mix well.

Cream Butter:
- In a separate large bowl, cream together the softened butter and vanilla extract until smooth.

Combine Wet and Dry Ingredients:
- Gradually add the dry ingredients to the wet ingredients, mixing until a soft dough forms. Ensure everything is well combined.

Shape Dough:
- Form the dough into a disc and wrap it in plastic wrap. Chill in the refrigerator for at least 30 minutes to firm up.

Roll and Cut Cookies:
- On a lightly floured surface or between two sheets of parchment paper, roll out the chilled dough to about 1/4-inch thickness. Use cookie cutters to cut out desired shapes.

Place on Baking Sheet:
- Place the cut-out cookies on the prepared baking sheet, leaving some space between each.

Bake:

- Bake in the preheated oven for 10-12 minutes or until the edges are lightly golden. Keep an eye on them to prevent over-baking.

Cool:
- Allow the cookies to cool on the baking sheet for a few minutes before transferring them to a wire rack to cool completely.

Enjoy:
- Once cooled, your Keto Lemon Almond Flour Shortbread Cookies are ready to be enjoyed! Store any leftovers in an airtight container.

These cookies are perfect for those on a low-carb or keto diet, and the lemon zest adds a refreshing twist to the classic shortbread flavor. Enjoy the buttery goodness!

Keto Chocolate Peanut Butter Cups

Ingredients:

For the Chocolate Layer:

- 4 oz (113g) sugar-free dark chocolate, chopped
- 2 tablespoons coconut oil

For the Peanut Butter Filling:

- 1/2 cup natural peanut butter (no added sugar)
- 2 tablespoons powdered erythritol or another keto-friendly sweetener
- 2 tablespoons coconut flour
- 2 tablespoons coconut oil, melted
- A pinch of salt

Instructions:

Prepare Muffin Tin:
- Line a muffin tin with paper cupcake liners.

Melt Chocolate:
- In a microwave-safe bowl or using a double boiler, melt the sugar-free dark chocolate and coconut oil together. Stir until smooth.

Coat the Bottom of Cups:
- Spoon a small amount of melted chocolate into the bottom of each cupcake liner, spreading it to cover the base.

Chill:
- Place the muffin tin in the freezer for about 10 minutes or until the chocolate layer is set.

Make Peanut Butter Filling:
- In a bowl, mix together natural peanut butter, powdered sweetener, coconut flour, melted coconut oil, and a pinch of salt. Stir until well combined.

Add Peanut Butter Layer:
- Spoon the peanut butter mixture over the chilled chocolate layer in each cup, smoothing it out.

Cover with Chocolate:

- Pour the remaining melted chocolate over the peanut butter layer, ensuring it covers the filling completely.

Chill Again:
- Place the muffin tin back in the freezer for another 15-20 minutes or until the chocolate is fully set.

Serve:
- Once set, your Keto Chocolate Peanut Butter Cups are ready to be enjoyed!

Store:
- Store any leftover cups in the refrigerator to maintain their firmness.

Feel free to customize this recipe by adding a sprinkle of sea salt on top or using almond butter instead of peanut butter for variation. These keto chocolate peanut butter cups are a delicious and satisfying treat without the excess carbs. Enjoy!

Coconut Flour Pumpkin Muffins

Ingredients:

Dry Ingredients:

- 1/2 cup coconut flour
- 1/2 teaspoon baking powder
- 1/2 teaspoon baking soda
- 1/2 teaspoon ground cinnamon
- 1/4 teaspoon ground nutmeg
- A pinch of salt

Wet Ingredients:

- 1/2 cup canned pumpkin puree
- 1/4 cup melted coconut oil
- 1/4 cup keto-friendly sweetener (e.g., erythritol or stevia)
- 3 large eggs
- 1 teaspoon vanilla extract

Optional Add-Ins:

- 1/4 cup chopped nuts (e.g., pecans or walnuts)
- Sugar-free chocolate chips (optional)

Instructions:

Preheat Oven:
- Preheat your oven to 350°F (175°C). Line a muffin tin with paper liners.

Mix Dry Ingredients:
- In a bowl, whisk together the coconut flour, baking powder, baking soda, ground cinnamon, ground nutmeg, and a pinch of salt. Ensure there are no lumps.

Combine Wet Ingredients:
- In a separate large bowl, whisk together the pumpkin puree, melted coconut oil, keto-friendly sweetener, eggs, and vanilla extract.

Combine Wet and Dry Ingredients:

- Add the dry ingredients to the wet ingredients and mix until well combined. Let the batter sit for a few minutes to allow the coconut flour to absorb the liquids.

Optional Add-Ins:
- If desired, fold in chopped nuts or sugar-free chocolate chips into the batter.

Fill Muffin Cups:
- Spoon the batter into the prepared muffin cups, filling each about 2/3 full.

Bake:
- Bake in the preheated oven for 18-22 minutes or until a toothpick inserted into the center of a muffin comes out clean.

Cool:
- Allow the muffins to cool in the tin for a few minutes, then transfer them to a wire rack to cool completely.

Serve:
- Once cooled, your Coconut Flour Pumpkin Muffins are ready to be enjoyed!

These muffins are a tasty and keto-friendly way to enjoy the warm, comforting flavors of pumpkin. Feel free to add your favorite low-carb toppings or enjoy them as is.

Chocolate Mint Keto Fat Bombs

Ingredients:

For the Chocolate Layer:

- 4 oz (113g) sugar-free dark chocolate, chopped
- 2 tablespoons coconut oil

For the Mint Filling:

- 1/2 cup coconut oil, melted
- 1/4 cup unsweetened shredded coconut
- 1/2 teaspoon peppermint extract
- 2 tablespoons powdered erythritol or another keto-friendly sweetener
- A pinch of salt
- Green food coloring (optional)

Instructions:

Prepare Molds:
- Line a mini muffin tin with paper liners or use silicone molds.

Make the Chocolate Layer:
- In a microwave-safe bowl or using a double boiler, melt the sugar-free dark chocolate and coconut oil together. Stir until smooth.

Coat Bottom of Molds:
- Spoon a small amount of melted chocolate into the bottom of each mold, spreading it to cover the base. Place the mold in the freezer for about 10 minutes to set.

Prepare the Mint Filling:
- In a bowl, mix together melted coconut oil, unsweetened shredded coconut, peppermint extract, powdered sweetener, and a pinch of salt. Add green food coloring if desired.

Add Mint Filling:
- Spoon the mint filling over the chilled chocolate layer in each mold, smoothing it out.

Cover with Chocolate:
- Pour the remaining melted chocolate over the mint filling, ensuring it covers the filling completely.

Chill:
- Place the mold back in the freezer for another 15-20 minutes or until the chocolate is fully set.

Serve:
- Once set, your Chocolate Mint Keto Fat Bombs are ready to be enjoyed!

Store:
- Store any leftover fat bombs in the refrigerator to maintain their firmness.

These fat bombs are not only delicious but also provide a healthy dose of fats to support your ketogenic lifestyle. Enjoy the cool and minty flavor combined with rich chocolate in these satisfying treats!

Vanilla Almond Flour Cupcakes

Ingredients:

For the Cupcakes:

- 2 cups almond flour
- 1/3 cup coconut flour
- 1 teaspoon baking powder
- 1/2 teaspoon baking soda
- 1/4 teaspoon salt
- 1/2 cup unsalted butter, softened
- 3/4 cup keto-friendly sweetener (e.g., erythritol or stevia)
- 4 large eggs
- 1/2 cup unsweetened almond milk
- 2 teaspoons vanilla extract

For the Frosting (Optional):

- 1/2 cup unsalted butter, softened
- 1 cup powdered erythritol or another keto-friendly sweetener
- 1 teaspoon vanilla extract
- 2-3 tablespoons heavy cream or coconut cream

Instructions:

Preheat Oven:
- Preheat your oven to 350°F (175°C). Line a muffin tin with cupcake liners.

Mix Dry Ingredients:
- In a bowl, whisk together almond flour, coconut flour, baking powder, baking soda, and salt. Ensure there are no lumps.

Cream Butter and Sweetener:
- In a separate large bowl, cream together softened butter and keto-friendly sweetener until light and fluffy.

Add Eggs:
- Add the eggs to the butter mixture one at a time, beating well after each addition.

Combine Wet and Dry Ingredients:

- Gradually add the dry ingredients to the wet ingredients, alternating with the almond milk. Begin and end with the dry ingredients. Mix until just combined.

Add Vanilla:
- Stir in the vanilla extract until evenly distributed.

Fill Cupcake Liners:
- Spoon the batter into the prepared cupcake liners, filling each about 2/3 full.

Bake:
- Bake in the preheated oven for 18-22 minutes or until a toothpick inserted into the center of a cupcake comes out clean.

Cool:
- Allow the cupcakes to cool in the tin for a few minutes before transferring them to a wire rack to cool completely.

Optional Frosting:
- If desired, prepare the frosting by creaming together softened butter, powdered sweetener, and vanilla extract. Add heavy cream or coconut cream until you achieve your desired consistency.

Frost and Serve:
- Once the cupcakes are completely cooled, frost them with the optional frosting or enjoy them as is.

These Vanilla Almond Flour Cupcakes are a delightful keto-friendly treat, perfect for satisfying your sweet cravings while keeping your carb intake low. Customize with your favorite frosting or enjoy them plain!

Keto Chocolate Macadamia Nut Cookies

Ingredients:

- 1 cup almond flour
- 1/4 cup coconut flour
- 1/3 cup unsweetened cocoa powder
- 1 teaspoon baking powder
- 1/4 teaspoon salt
- 1/2 cup unsalted butter, softened
- 1/2 cup keto-friendly sweetener (e.g., erythritol or stevia)
- 1 large egg
- 1 teaspoon vanilla extract
- 1/2 cup chopped macadamia nuts
- 1/4 cup sugar-free chocolate chips (optional)

Instructions:

Preheat Oven:
- Preheat your oven to 350°F (175°C). Line a baking sheet with parchment paper.

Mix Dry Ingredients:
- In a bowl, whisk together almond flour, coconut flour, cocoa powder, baking powder, and salt. Ensure there are no lumps.

Cream Butter and Sweetener:
- In a separate large bowl, cream together softened butter and keto-friendly sweetener until light and fluffy.

Add Egg and Vanilla:
- Add the egg and vanilla extract to the butter mixture. Beat until well combined.

Combine Wet and Dry Ingredients:
- Gradually add the dry ingredients to the wet ingredients, mixing until just combined.

Fold in Macadamia Nuts and Chocolate Chips:
- Gently fold in the chopped macadamia nuts and sugar-free chocolate chips into the cookie dough.

Scoop and Shape:
- Using a cookie scoop or tablespoon, drop rounded portions of dough onto the prepared baking sheet. Space them about 2 inches apart.

Bake:

- Bake in the preheated oven for 10-12 minutes or until the edges are set. The cookies may seem soft, but they will firm up as they cool.

Cool:
- Allow the cookies to cool on the baking sheet for a few minutes, then transfer them to a wire rack to cool completely.

Serve:
- Once cooled, your Keto Chocolate Macadamia Nut Cookies are ready to be enjoyed!

These cookies are a delightful treat for chocolate and nut lovers on a keto or low-carb diet. Enjoy them with a cup of your favorite low-carb beverage!

Avocado Lime Keto Cheesecake

Ingredients:

For the Crust:

- 1 1/2 cups almond flour
- 1/4 cup melted unsalted butter
- 2 tablespoons powdered erythritol or another keto-friendly sweetener
- A pinch of salt

For the Filling:

- 3 ripe avocados, peeled and pitted
- 16 oz (450g) cream cheese, softened
- 3/4 cup powdered erythritol or another keto-friendly sweetener
- Zest and juice of 2 limes
- 1 teaspoon vanilla extract
- A pinch of salt

For Topping (Optional):

- Whipped cream
- Lime slices for garnish

Instructions:

Preheat Oven:
- Preheat your oven to 325°F (163°C). Grease a springform pan.

Make the Crust:
- In a bowl, combine almond flour, melted butter, powdered sweetener, and a pinch of salt. Press the mixture into the bottom of the prepared pan to form the crust.

Bake the Crust:
- Bake the crust in the preheated oven for 10-12 minutes or until it's lightly golden. Remove from the oven and let it cool.

Prepare the Filling:

- In a food processor or blender, combine peeled and pitted avocados, softened cream cheese, powdered sweetener, lime zest, lime juice, vanilla extract, and a pinch of salt. Blend until smooth and creamy.

Pour Filling into Crust:
- Pour the avocado lime filling over the cooled crust in the springform pan, spreading it evenly.

Smooth the Top:
- Use a spatula to smooth the top of the cheesecake filling.

Chill:
- Place the cheesecake in the refrigerator and let it chill for at least 4 hours or overnight to set.

Serve:
- Once the cheesecake is set, remove it from the springform pan. Optionally, top with whipped cream and garnish with lime slices.

Slice and Enjoy:
- Slice your Avocado Lime Keto Cheesecake and enjoy this refreshing and creamy dessert!

This cheesecake is not only keto-friendly but also rich in healthy fats from avocados. It's a perfect treat for those on a low-carb or ketogenic diet.

Peanut Butter Chocolate Chip Keto Blondies

Ingredients:

- 1 cup almond flour
- 1/3 cup coconut flour
- 1/2 cup unsalted butter, melted
- 1/2 cup natural peanut butter (no added sugar)
- 3/4 cup powdered erythritol or another keto-friendly sweetener
- 2 large eggs
- 1 teaspoon vanilla extract
- 1/2 teaspoon baking powder
- A pinch of salt
- 1/2 cup sugar-free chocolate chips

Instructions:

Preheat Oven:
- Preheat your oven to 350°F (175°C). Grease or line a baking pan (8x8 inches) with parchment paper.

Mix Dry Ingredients:
- In a bowl, whisk together almond flour, coconut flour, baking powder, and a pinch of salt. Ensure there are no lumps.

Combine Wet Ingredients:
- In a separate large bowl, combine melted butter, natural peanut butter, powdered sweetener, eggs, and vanilla extract. Mix until well combined.

Combine Wet and Dry Ingredients:
- Gradually add the dry ingredients to the wet ingredients, mixing until just combined.

Fold in Chocolate Chips:
- Gently fold in the sugar-free chocolate chips into the blondie batter.

Transfer to Baking Pan:
- Transfer the batter to the prepared baking pan, spreading it evenly.

Bake:
- Bake in the preheated oven for 20-25 minutes or until the edges are golden and a toothpick inserted into the center comes out clean or with a few moist crumbs.

Cool:
- Allow the blondies to cool in the pan for at least 10 minutes before transferring them to a wire rack to cool completely.

Slice and Serve:
- Once cooled, slice the Peanut Butter Chocolate Chip Keto Blondies into squares and enjoy!

These blondies are a delightful combination of peanut butter and chocolate without the added carbs. Perfect for satisfying your sweet cravings on a keto or low-carb diet!

Almond Flour Berry Cobbler

Ingredients:

For the Berry Filling:

- 3 cups mixed berries (strawberries, blueberries, raspberries, blackberries)
- 1/4 cup powdered erythritol or another keto-friendly sweetener
- 1 tablespoon lemon juice
- Zest of 1 lemon
- 1 tablespoon almond flour (for thickening)

For the Almond Flour Topping:

- 1 cup almond flour
- 1/4 cup powdered erythritol or another keto-friendly sweetener
- 1 teaspoon baking powder
- A pinch of salt
- 1/4 cup unsalted butter, melted
- 1 teaspoon vanilla extract
- 1/4 cup unsweetened almond milk

Instructions:

Preheat Oven:
- Preheat your oven to 350°F (175°C).

Prepare Berry Filling:
- In a mixing bowl, combine the mixed berries, powdered sweetener, lemon juice, lemon zest, and 1 tablespoon of almond flour. Toss the berries until they are well coated.

Transfer to Baking Dish:
- Transfer the berry mixture to a greased baking dish, spreading it evenly.

Make Almond Flour Topping:
- In another bowl, whisk together almond flour, powdered sweetener, baking powder, and a pinch of salt.

Add Wet Ingredients:
- Stir in melted butter, vanilla extract, and unsweetened almond milk to the almond flour mixture. Mix until well combined.

Drop Topping onto Berries:

- Drop spoonfuls of the almond flour topping onto the berry mixture, covering it as evenly as possible.

Bake:
- Bake in the preheated oven for 25-30 minutes or until the topping is golden brown and the berries are bubbling.

Cool:
- Allow the cobbler to cool for a few minutes before serving.

Serve:
- Serve the Almond Flour Berry Cobbler warm, optionally with a dollop of keto-friendly whipped cream or a scoop of sugar-free vanilla ice cream.

This Almond Flour Berry Cobbler is a delightful and guilt-free dessert, perfect for those on a keto or low-carb diet. Enjoy the fruity goodness with the nutty almond flour topping!

Keto Chocolate Mint Ice Cream

Ingredients:

- 2 cups heavy cream
- 1 cup unsweetened almond milk
- 3/4 cup powdered erythritol or another keto-friendly sweetener
- 1/3 cup unsweetened cocoa powder
- 1 teaspoon peppermint extract
- 1/2 teaspoon vanilla extract
- A pinch of salt
- Sugar-free chocolate chips (optional)

Instructions:

Prepare Ice Cream Maker:
- If you have an ice cream maker, ensure the freezer bowl is frozen according to the manufacturer's instructions. If not, you can still make this recipe by placing the mixture in the freezer and stirring periodically.

Mix Ingredients:
- In a mixing bowl, whisk together heavy cream, almond milk, powdered sweetener, cocoa powder, peppermint extract, vanilla extract, and a pinch of salt. Make sure the sweetener is fully dissolved.

Chill Mixture:
- Cover the bowl and refrigerate the mixture for at least 2 hours, or until it's well chilled.

Ice Cream Maker Method:
- Pour the chilled mixture into your ice cream maker and churn according to the manufacturer's instructions. Add sugar-free chocolate chips during the last few minutes of churning, if desired.

Freezer Method:
- If you don't have an ice cream maker, pour the chilled mixture into a shallow dish and place it in the freezer. Stir the mixture every 30 minutes for the first 2-3 hours to prevent ice crystals from forming. Add sugar-free chocolate chips during one of the stirring sessions.

Freeze:
- Once the ice cream reaches your desired consistency, transfer it to a lidded container and freeze for an additional 2-4 hours or until firm.

Serve:
- Scoop the Keto Chocolate Mint Ice Cream into bowls or cones and enjoy!

This minty chocolate ice cream is a delightful treat for those following a ketogenic or low-carb diet. Customize it to your liking and savor the cool and creamy goodness!

Coconut Flour Chocolate Mug Cake

Ingredients:

- 2 tablespoons coconut flour
- 2 tablespoons unsweetened cocoa powder
- 2 tablespoons powdered erythritol or another keto-friendly sweetener
- 1/4 teaspoon baking powder
- A pinch of salt
- 2 tablespoons melted unsalted butter
- 1/4 cup unsweetened almond milk
- 1/2 teaspoon vanilla extract
- 1 large egg
- Sugar-free chocolate chips (optional, for extra indulgence)

Instructions:

Prepare Mug:
- Grease a microwave-safe mug with a bit of butter or cooking spray.

Mix Dry Ingredients:
- In a small bowl, whisk together coconut flour, cocoa powder, powdered sweetener, baking powder, and a pinch of salt.

Combine Wet Ingredients:
- In the mug, add melted butter, unsweetened almond milk, vanilla extract, and the egg. Whisk until well combined.

Mix Batter:
- Gradually add the dry ingredients to the wet ingredients in the mug, stirring well to avoid lumps. Ensure the batter is smooth and evenly mixed.

Optional Chocolate Chips:
- If desired, fold in a few sugar-free chocolate chips into the batter.

Microwave:
- Microwave the mug on high for 1.5 to 2 minutes. The cooking time may vary depending on your microwave's wattage. The cake should rise and set.

Cool:
- Allow the mug cake to cool for a few minutes before digging in.

Optional Toppings:
- Top the Coconut Flour Chocolate Mug Cake with whipped cream, a sprinkle of cocoa powder, or more chocolate chips if you like.

Enjoy:

- Grab a spoon and enjoy your quick and delicious Coconut Flour Chocolate Mug Cake!

This single-serving dessert is perfect for those on a keto or low-carb diet who want a sweet treat without the guilt. Adjust the sweetness and add-ins to suit your taste preferences!

Keto Pumpkin Spice Fat Bombs

Ingredients:

- 1/2 cup canned pumpkin puree
- 1/4 cup coconut oil, melted
- 1/4 cup unsalted butter, softened
- 2 tablespoons powdered erythritol or another keto-friendly sweetener
- 1 teaspoon pumpkin pie spice
- 1/2 teaspoon vanilla extract
- A pinch of salt

Instructions:

Mix Ingredients:
- In a bowl, combine canned pumpkin puree, melted coconut oil, softened butter, powdered sweetener, pumpkin pie spice, vanilla extract, and a pinch of salt. Mix until well combined.

Chill Mixture:
- Place the mixture in the refrigerator for about 30 minutes to firm up slightly. This will make it easier to shape into fat bombs.

Shape Fat Bombs:
- Once the mixture has chilled, use a spoon or a small cookie scoop to shape it into small balls. Place the balls on a parchment paper-lined tray.

Optional Coating:
- For an extra touch, you can roll the fat bombs in additional pumpkin pie spice or finely chopped nuts.

Chill Again:
- Place the tray in the refrigerator for at least 1-2 hours or until the fat bombs are firm.

Serve and Enjoy:
- Once the Pumpkin Spice Fat Bombs are set, transfer them to an airtight container and store in the refrigerator. Enjoy as a satisfying treat when you need a little energy boost!

These fat bombs are rich in healthy fats and have the delightful flavors of pumpkin spice. They are not only delicious but also a great way to meet your daily fat intake on a keto diet. Enjoy!

Raspberry Almond Flour Scones

Ingredients:

For the Scones:

- 2 cups almond flour
- 1/4 cup coconut flour
- 1/4 cup powdered erythritol or another keto-friendly sweetener
- 1 teaspoon baking powder
- 1/4 teaspoon salt
- 1/4 cup unsalted butter, chilled and cubed
- 1/4 cup heavy cream
- 1 large egg
- 1 teaspoon almond extract
- 1/2 cup fresh raspberries

For the Glaze (Optional):

- 1/4 cup powdered erythritol
- 1 tablespoon almond milk
- 1/4 teaspoon almond extract

Instructions:

Preheat Oven:
- Preheat your oven to 350°F (175°C). Line a baking sheet with parchment paper.

Mix Dry Ingredients:
- In a large bowl, whisk together almond flour, coconut flour, powdered sweetener, baking powder, and salt.

Cut in Butter:
- Add the chilled and cubed butter to the dry ingredients. Use a pastry cutter or your fingers to cut the butter into the flour until the mixture resembles coarse crumbs.

Combine Wet Ingredients:
- In a separate bowl, whisk together heavy cream, egg, and almond extract.

Combine Wet and Dry Ingredients:
- Pour the wet ingredients into the dry ingredients and stir until just combined. Be careful not to overmix.

Fold in Raspberries:
- Gently fold in the fresh raspberries, being careful not to crush them too much.

Shape Scones:
- Transfer the dough to a floured surface and shape it into a circle about 1 inch thick. Cut the circle into 8 wedges.

Bake:
- Place the scones on the prepared baking sheet and bake in the preheated oven for 18-22 minutes or until the edges are golden brown.

Prepare Glaze (Optional):
- If desired, mix together the powdered erythritol, almond milk, and almond extract to make a glaze. Drizzle it over the cooled scones.

Serve and Enjoy:
- Allow the Raspberry Almond Flour Scones to cool slightly before serving. Enjoy with your favorite keto-friendly beverage!

These scones are a delicious and satisfying option for those on a keto or low-carb diet. The almond flour provides a rich and nutty flavor, while the raspberries add a burst of sweetness.

Keto Chocolate Avocado Truffles

Ingredients:

- 1 ripe avocado, peeled and pitted
- 4 oz (113g) sugar-free dark chocolate, chopped
- 2 tablespoons unsweetened cocoa powder
- 2 tablespoons powdered erythritol or another keto-friendly sweetener
- 1/2 teaspoon vanilla extract
- A pinch of salt
- Optional coatings: unsweetened shredded coconut, chopped nuts, or additional cocoa powder

Instructions:

Prepare Avocado:
- In a food processor, blend the ripe avocado until smooth and creamy. You can also use a fork to mash it thoroughly.

Melt Chocolate:
- In a microwave-safe bowl or using a double boiler, melt the sugar-free dark chocolate until smooth.

Combine Ingredients:
- Add the melted chocolate, cocoa powder, powdered sweetener, vanilla extract, and a pinch of salt to the mashed avocado. Blend or mix until well combined.

Chill Mixture:
- Place the mixture in the refrigerator for at least 30 minutes to allow it to firm up.

Shape Truffles:
- Once the mixture is firm, scoop out small portions and shape them into balls to form truffles. You can use a spoon or your hands for this step.

Coat Truffles (Optional):
- Roll the truffles in unsweetened shredded coconut, chopped nuts, or additional cocoa powder for a coating. This step is optional but adds extra flavor and texture.

Chill Again:
- Place the coated truffles on a parchment-lined tray and chill in the refrigerator for an additional 30 minutes to set.

Serve and Enjoy:

- Once set, your Keto Chocolate Avocado Truffles are ready to be enjoyed! Keep them refrigerated until serving.

These truffles are a delicious way to incorporate the creamy goodness of avocados into a sweet treat while keeping it keto-friendly. Enjoy the rich and velvety texture of these chocolate delights!

Almond Butter Keto Chocolate Fudge

Ingredients:

- 1 cup unsweetened almond butter
- 1/2 cup coconut oil
- 1/4 cup unsweetened cocoa powder
- 1/4 cup powdered erythritol or another keto-friendly sweetener
- 1 teaspoon vanilla extract
- A pinch of salt
- Optional: Chopped almonds or unsweetened shredded coconut for topping

Instructions:

Prepare a Pan:
- Line a small square baking dish or pan with parchment paper, leaving some overhang for easy removal.

Melt Almond Butter and Coconut Oil:
- In a saucepan over low heat or in the microwave, melt the almond butter and coconut oil until smooth and well combined.

Add Cocoa Powder and Sweetener:
- Remove the mixture from heat and whisk in the unsweetened cocoa powder, powdered sweetener, vanilla extract, and a pinch of salt. Ensure the sweetener is fully dissolved.

Mix Well:
- Stir the mixture until it becomes a smooth and glossy chocolate fudge mixture.

Pour into Pan:
- Pour the chocolate fudge mixture into the prepared pan, spreading it out evenly.

Optional Toppings:
- If desired, sprinkle chopped almonds or unsweetened shredded coconut over the top of the fudge.

Chill:
- Place the pan in the refrigerator and let the fudge set for at least 2-3 hours or until firm.

Slice:
- Once the fudge is set, use the parchment paper overhang to lift it out of the pan. Place it on a cutting board and slice it into small squares.

Serve and Enjoy:

- Your Almond Butter Keto Chocolate Fudge is ready to be enjoyed! Store any leftovers in the refrigerator.

This creamy and nutty fudge is a delightful way to satisfy your sweet tooth on a keto or low-carb diet. Enjoy the rich flavors and the velvety texture of this guilt-free treat!

Blueberry Coconut Flour Pancakes

Ingredients:

- 1/4 cup coconut flour
- 1/2 teaspoon baking powder
- Pinch of salt
- 3 large eggs
- 1/4 cup unsweetened almond milk or coconut milk
- 2 tablespoons melted coconut oil or butter
- 1 tablespoon powdered erythritol or another keto-friendly sweetener
- 1/2 teaspoon vanilla extract
- 1/2 cup fresh blueberries
- Additional coconut oil or butter for cooking

Instructions:

Mix Dry Ingredients:
- In a bowl, whisk together coconut flour, baking powder, and a pinch of salt.

Combine Wet Ingredients:
- In a separate bowl, whisk together eggs, almond milk, melted coconut oil or butter, powdered sweetener, and vanilla extract.

Combine Wet and Dry Ingredients:
- Add the wet ingredients to the dry ingredients and stir until well combined. Allow the batter to sit for a few minutes to let the coconut flour absorb the liquids.

Fold in Blueberries:
- Gently fold in the fresh blueberries into the pancake batter.

Preheat Pan:
- Heat a griddle or non-stick skillet over medium heat. Add a small amount of coconut oil or butter to grease the surface.

Scoop Batter:
- Using a ladle or measuring cup, scoop portions of the batter onto the preheated griddle to form pancakes.

Cook Until Bubbles:
- Cook until small bubbles form on the surface of the pancakes, then flip and cook the other side until golden brown.

Repeat:
- Repeat the process until all the batter is used, adding more coconut oil or butter to the griddle as needed.

Serve and Enjoy:
- Serve the Blueberry Coconut Flour Pancakes warm. Optionally, top with additional fresh blueberries, a dollop of whipped cream, or a drizzle of sugar-free maple syrup.

These pancakes are a delicious and nutritious way to start your day while keeping your carb intake low. Enjoy the burst of blueberry flavor and the subtle coconut undertones in every bite!

Keto Almond Flour Waffles

Ingredients:

- 1 1/2 cups almond flour
- 1/4 cup coconut flour
- 2 tablespoons powdered erythritol or another keto-friendly sweetener
- 1 teaspoon baking powder
- 1/4 teaspoon salt
- 4 large eggs
- 1/2 cup unsweetened almond milk
- 1/4 cup unsalted butter, melted
- 1 teaspoon vanilla extract

Instructions:

Preheat Waffle Iron:
- Preheat your waffle iron according to the manufacturer's instructions.

Mix Dry Ingredients:
- In a large bowl, whisk together almond flour, coconut flour, powdered sweetener, baking powder, and salt.

Combine Wet Ingredients:
- In another bowl, beat the eggs. Add almond milk, melted butter, and vanilla extract. Mix well.

Combine Wet and Dry Ingredients:
- Pour the wet ingredients into the bowl with the dry ingredients. Stir until well combined. The batter should be thick but pourable. If it's too thick, you can add a bit more almond milk.

Grease Waffle Iron:
- Lightly grease the waffle iron with non-stick cooking spray or a small amount of melted butter.

Cook Waffles:
- Spoon the batter onto the preheated waffle iron, spreading it evenly. Cook according to the manufacturer's instructions until the waffles are golden brown and crisp.

Serve:
- Carefully remove the waffles from the iron and repeat with the remaining batter. Serve the keto almond flour waffles warm.

Optional Toppings:

- Top your waffles with keto-friendly toppings such as sugar-free syrup, whipped cream, berries, or a dollop of almond butter.

These almond flour waffles are a tasty and satisfying option for those on a keto or low-carb diet. They provide a great way to enjoy a classic breakfast while keeping your carb intake low. Customize with your favorite toppings and enjoy!

Chocolate Coconut Flour Cupcakes

Ingredients:

For the Cupcakes:

- 1/2 cup coconut flour
- 1/4 cup unsweetened cocoa powder
- 1/2 teaspoon baking powder
- 1/4 teaspoon baking soda
- A pinch of salt
- 1/2 cup unsalted butter, softened
- 1/2 cup powdered erythritol or another keto-friendly sweetener
- 4 large eggs
- 1/2 cup unsweetened almond milk
- 1 teaspoon vanilla extract

For the Frosting:

- 1/2 cup unsalted butter, softened
- 1/4 cup powdered erythritol or another keto-friendly sweetener
- 2 tablespoons unsweetened cocoa powder
- 1/2 teaspoon vanilla extract
- 2-3 tablespoons heavy cream or coconut cream

Optional Toppings:

- Shredded coconut or grated dark chocolate

Instructions:

Preheat Oven:
- Preheat your oven to 350°F (175°C). Line a muffin tin with cupcake liners.

Mix Dry Ingredients:
- In a bowl, whisk together coconut flour, cocoa powder, baking powder, baking soda, and a pinch of salt. Ensure there are no lumps.

Cream Butter and Sweetener:
- In a separate large bowl, cream together softened butter and powdered sweetener until light and fluffy.

Add Eggs:
- Add the eggs to the butter mixture one at a time, beating well after each addition.

Combine Wet and Dry Ingredients:
- Gradually add the dry ingredients to the wet ingredients, alternating with the almond milk. Begin and end with the dry ingredients. Mix until just combined.

Add Vanilla:
- Stir in the vanilla extract until evenly distributed.

Fill Cupcake Liners:
- Spoon the batter into the prepared cupcake liners, filling each about 2/3 full.

Bake:
- Bake in the preheated oven for 18-22 minutes or until a toothpick inserted into the center of a cupcake comes out clean.

Cool:
- Allow the cupcakes to cool in the tin for a few minutes before transferring them to a wire rack to cool completely.

Prepare Frosting:
- While the cupcakes are cooling, prepare the frosting by creaming together softened butter, powdered sweetener, cocoa powder, and vanilla extract. Add heavy cream or coconut cream until you achieve your desired consistency.

Frost Cupcakes:
- Once the cupcakes are completely cooled, frost them with the chocolate coconut frosting.

Optional Toppings:
- Sprinkle shredded coconut or grated dark chocolate on top for an extra touch.

These Chocolate Coconut Flour Cupcakes are a delightful keto-friendly treat. Enjoy the rich and moist texture with a delicious chocolate coconut frosting!

Keto Lemon Coconut Fat Bombs

Ingredients:

- 1/2 cup coconut oil, melted
- 1/2 cup unsweetened shredded coconut
- 3 tablespoons powdered erythritol or another keto-friendly sweetener
- Zest of 1 lemon
- 2 tablespoons lemon juice
- 1/2 teaspoon vanilla extract
- A pinch of salt

Instructions:

Mix Ingredients:
- In a bowl, combine melted coconut oil, shredded coconut, powdered sweetener, lemon zest, lemon juice, vanilla extract, and a pinch of salt. Mix well.

Chill Mixture:
- Place the mixture in the refrigerator for about 30 minutes to firm up slightly. This will make it easier to shape into fat bombs.

Shape Fat Bombs:
- Once the mixture has chilled, use a spoon or a small cookie scoop to shape it into small balls to form fat bombs. Place the balls on a parchment paper-lined tray.

Optional Coating:
- For an extra touch, you can roll the fat bombs in additional shredded coconut.

Chill Again:
- Place the tray in the refrigerator for at least 1-2 hours or until the fat bombs are firm.

Serve and Enjoy:
- Once the Lemon Coconut Fat Bombs are set, transfer them to an airtight container and store in the refrigerator. Enjoy as a satisfying and citrusy treat when you need a little energy boost!

These fat bombs are a tasty and convenient way to add healthy fats to your diet while staying in ketosis. The combination of lemon and coconut provides a refreshing flavor that's perfect for a quick snack or dessert. Enjoy!

Pumpkin Pie Keto Chia Pudding

Ingredients:

- 1/4 cup chia seeds
- 1 cup unsweetened almond milk or coconut milk
- 1/4 cup pumpkin puree
- 2 tablespoons powdered erythritol or another keto-friendly sweetener
- 1/2 teaspoon pumpkin pie spice
- 1/2 teaspoon vanilla extract
- A pinch of salt
- Whipped cream (optional, for topping)

Instructions:

Mix Chia Seeds and Liquid:
- In a bowl, combine chia seeds and almond milk. Stir well to ensure the chia seeds are evenly distributed.

Add Pumpkin and Sweetener:
- Add the pumpkin puree, powdered sweetener, pumpkin pie spice, vanilla extract, and a pinch of salt to the chia seed mixture. Mix thoroughly.

Chill:
- Cover the bowl and refrigerate the mixture for at least 2-3 hours or overnight. This allows the chia seeds to absorb the liquid and create a pudding-like consistency.

Stir Again:
- After the initial chilling period, stir the mixture again to make sure the chia seeds are evenly distributed.

Chill Further:
- Return the mixture to the refrigerator for an additional 1-2 hours or until the chia pudding reaches your desired thickness.

Serve:
- Once the Pumpkin Pie Keto Chia Pudding is set, give it a final stir and portion it into serving bowls or jars.

Top with Whipped Cream (Optional):
- If desired, top the chia pudding with a dollop of keto-friendly whipped cream just before serving.

Enjoy:
- Enjoy your Pumpkin Pie Keto Chia Pudding as a satisfying and seasonal treat!

This chia pudding combines the warmth of pumpkin pie spice with the creamy texture of chia seeds, making it a delightful and keto-friendly option for fall. Feel free to customize the sweetness and adjust the spices to suit your taste preferences.

Almond Flour Keto Cinnamon Rolls

Ingredients:

For the Dough:

- 2 cups almond flour
- 1/4 cup coconut flour
- 1/4 cup powdered erythritol or another keto-friendly sweetener
- 1 teaspoon baking powder
- 1/2 teaspoon xanthan gum (optional, for texture)
- A pinch of salt
- 1/4 cup unsalted butter, melted
- 2 large eggs
- 1 teaspoon vanilla extract

For the Filling:

- 1/4 cup unsalted butter, softened
- 2 tablespoons powdered erythritol
- 1 tablespoon ground cinnamon

For the Cream Cheese Frosting:

- 4 oz (113g) cream cheese, softened
- 1/4 cup unsalted butter, softened
- 1/4 cup powdered erythritol
- 1 teaspoon vanilla extract

Instructions:

Preheat Oven:
- Preheat your oven to 350°F (175°C). Grease a baking dish or line it with parchment paper.

Make the Dough:
- In a large bowl, whisk together almond flour, coconut flour, powdered sweetener, baking powder, xanthan gum (if using), and a pinch of salt.

Add Wet Ingredients:
- Stir in melted butter, eggs, and vanilla extract. Mix until a dough forms.

Roll Out the Dough:
- Place the dough between two sheets of parchment paper and roll it out into a rectangle, about 1/4 inch thick.

Spread Filling:
- In a small bowl, mix together softened butter, powdered sweetener, and ground cinnamon. Spread this mixture evenly over the rolled-out dough.

Roll Up the Dough:
- Carefully roll up the dough, starting from one of the longer edges.

Slice Rolls:
- Use a sharp knife to slice the rolled-up dough into individual cinnamon rolls.

Place in Baking Dish:
- Place the cinnamon rolls in the prepared baking dish.

Bake:
- Bake in the preheated oven for 15-20 minutes or until the rolls are golden brown.

Make Cream Cheese Frosting:
- While the rolls are baking, prepare the cream cheese frosting. In a bowl, beat together softened cream cheese, butter, powdered sweetener, and vanilla extract until smooth.

Frost Cinnamon Rolls:
- Once the rolls are done baking and have cooled slightly, spread the cream cheese frosting over the top.

Serve and Enjoy:
- Serve your Almond Flour Keto Cinnamon Rolls warm and enjoy this delicious low-carb treat!

These cinnamon rolls are a delightful and keto-friendly alternative to the traditional version. The almond flour provides a nutty flavor, and the cream cheese frosting adds a rich and creamy touch. Enjoy!

www.ingramcontent.com/pod-product-compliance
Lightning Source LLC
LaVergne TN
LVHW081606060526
838201LV00054B/2103